MOTIVATION

ɹotations to inspire and celebrate the spirit of excellence

Compiled by Dan Zadra
Designed by Kobi Yamada
and Steve Potter

COM·PEN·DI·UM™
Publishing

LYNNWOOD, WASHINGTON

ACKNOWLEDGEMENTS
These quotations were gathered lovingly but
unscientifically over several years and/or
contributed by many friends or acquaintances.
Some arrived, and survived in our files, on
scraps of paper and may therefore be
imperfectly worded or attributed. To the
authors, contributors and original sources, our
thanks, and where appropriate, our apologies.
—The editors

CREDITS
Compiled by Dan Zadra
Designed by Kobi Yamada and Steve Potter

ISBN 1-888387-96-3

MOTIVATION

A Gift to Inspire and Celebrate
Your Achievements

*Encourage each other
to become the best you can be.*
—Tom Peters

Everyone seems to have a favorite
thought or treasured quotation tucked
away like a little island in a quiet part
of the mind. In times of stress or
pressure, we return to these thoughts
again and again. They remind us that
our possibilities are always bigger than
our problems. At our best, we can
do more than dream, we can imagine.
We can do more than work, we can
grow. We can do more criticize, we

can encourage. We can do more than endure, we can prevail.

The following pages are alive with nearly 200 motivational thoughts, a unique collection from some of the world's most accomplished and creative people. Most of these insights average fewer than 35 words each, making them easy to remember and pass along to others. We hope you'll enjoy every thought, and that you'll share your favorites with friends, colleagues, customers or teammates.

Here's to your continuing success. May this book be a source of inspiration and joy for you—just as your work, dreams and accomplishments are an inspiration for others.

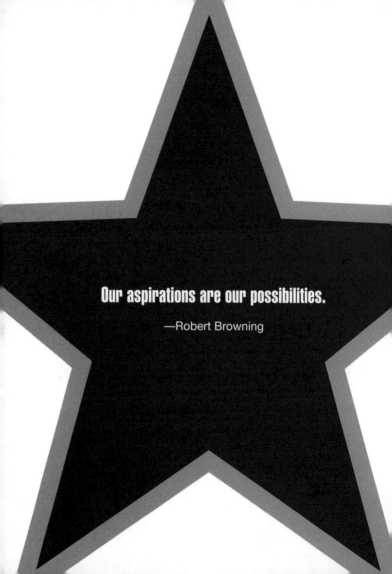

Our aspirations are our possibilities.

—Robert Browning

It may be those who
do most, dream most.

STEPHEN LEACOCK

Nothing much
happens without a dream.
For something really great
to happen, it takes a
really great dream.

ROBERT GREENLEAF

If we did all the
things we are capable of,
we would literally
astound ourselves.

THOMAS EDISON

Too low they build
who build below
the skies.

EDWARD YOUNG

There is nothing
like a dream to
create the future.

VICTOR HUGO

What great thing
would you attempt if
you knew you could not fail?

ROBERT SCHULLER

Self-confidence
is the first requisite
to great undertakings.

DR. SAMUEL JOHNSON

No one rises to low
expectations.

LES BROWN

Limited expectations
yield only limited results.

SUSAN LAURSON WILLIG

Try to dream high enough
to lose the dream in
the seeking of it.

WILLIAM FAULKNER

I was restless. I was doing okay, but I was restless. One day it dawned on me that I had been looking at life through the wrong end of the telescope. It was up to me to turn it around to make it bigger, better, more satisfying.

ARNOLD SWARZENEGGER

You have to think anyway, so why not think big?

DONALD TRUMP

I dare you,
while there is still time
to have a magnificent
obsession.

WILLIAM DANFORTH

The greatest achievement
was at first and for a time
only a dream.

JAMES ALLEN

The beginning is always today.

—Mary Wollstonecraft

All glory comes
from daring to begin.

EUGENE WARE

The first step towards
getting somewhere is to
decide that you are not going
to stay where you are.

J. PIERPONT MORGAN

You must take your chance.

WILLIAM SHAKESPEARE

★

You may be disappointed
if you fail, but you are
doomed if you don't try.

BEVERLY SILLS

To change your life,
start immediately, do it
flamboyantly, no exceptions,
no excuses.

WILLIAM JAMES

If you have a great ambition,
take as big a step as possible
in the direction of fulfilling it.

MILDRED MCAFEE

Do the thing and
you will have the power.

RALPH WALDO EMERSON

A rock pile ceases to be
a rock pile the moment a
single man contemplates it,
bearing within him the
image of a cathedral.

ANTOINE DE SAINT-EXUPERY

The minute you
begin to do what you
really want to do, it's really
a different kind of life.

BUCKMINSTER R. FULLER

No journey is too great if you
find what you seek.

UNKNOWN

Think of something
that would be "wonderful"
if it were only "possible."
Then set out to make
it possible.

ARMAND HAMMER

From small beginnings
come great things.

PROVERB

He who chooses the beginning of a road, also chooses its destination.

STEVE FULLER

Set your course by the stars, not by the lights of every passing ship.

GEN. OMAR BRADLEY

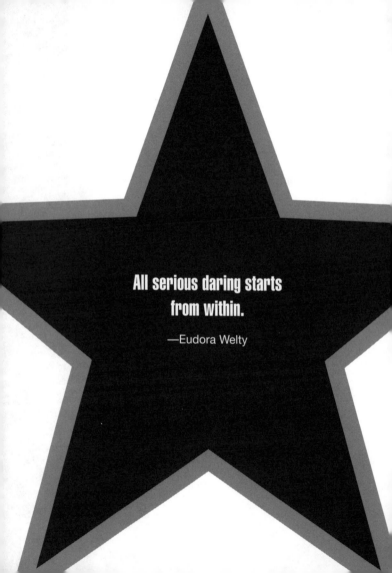

**All serious daring starts
from within.**

—Eudora Welty

We must dare, and dare again, and go on daring.

GEORGE JACQUES DANTON

Sometimes you just have to take the leap, and build your wings on the way down.

KOBI YAMADA

It is not because
things are difficult that
we do not dare; it is
because we do not dare
that things are difficult.

SENECA

Life expects something of you,
and it is up to every individual
to discover what it should be.

VICTOR FRANKL

A life not put to the test
is not worth living.

EPICTECUS

Being courageous requires
no exceptional qualifications,
no magic formula, no special
combination of time, place
and circumstance. It is an
opportunity that sooner or
later is presented to us all.

JOHN F. KENNEDY

Everyone has the
right to risk his own life
in order to save it.

JEAN-JACQUES ROUSSEAU

★

There is the risk
you cannot afford to take,
and there is the risk
you cannot afford not to take.

PETER DRUCKER

Taking chances
helps you grow.

UNKNOWN

What people say you
cannot do, you try and
find that you can.

HENRY DAVID THOREAU

Daring ideas are like chessmen moved forward. They may be beaten, but they may start a winning game.

JOHANN WOLFGANG VON GOETHE

Sometimes taking a risk is the safest thing to do.

MERYL WILLIAMS

If you play it safe in life
you've decided that you don't
want to grow anymore.

SHIRLEY HUFSTEFLER

Do you want to be safe and
good, or do you want to take
a chance and be great?

JIMMY JOHNSON

Until you try, you don't know what you can do.

HENRY JAMES

★

Most of the things worth doing in the world had been declared impossible before they were done.

LOUIS BRANDEIS

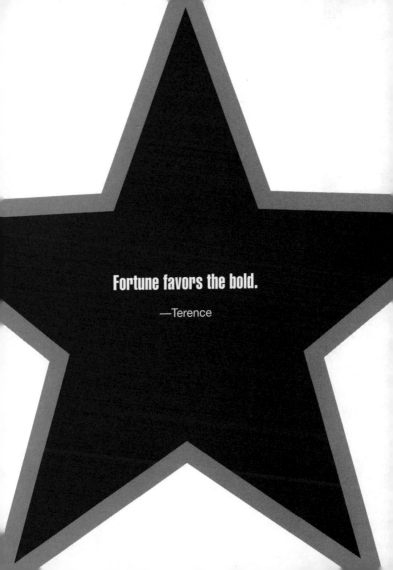

Fortune favors the bold.

—Terence

Discipline is the whole key
to being successful. We all
get 24 hours a day. It's the
only fair thing; it's the only thing
that's equal. It's up to us
as to what we do with
those 24 hours.

SAM HUFF

Each day comes to
me with both hands
full of possibilities.

HELEN KELLER

I've found that luck is quite predictable. If you want more luck, take more chances. Be more active. Show up more often.

BRIAN TRACY

I'm a great believer in luck, and I find the harder I work, the more I have of it.

DAVID PRESCOTT

People will try to tell you
that all the great opportunities
have been snapped up.
In reality, the world changes
every second, blowing new
opportunities in all directions,
including yours.

KEN HAKUTA

Opportunities multiply as
they are seized.

JOHN WICKER

All things are what
you make them.

PLAUTUS

When you hold back on life,
life holds back on you.

MARY MANIN MORRISSEY

Almost everything comes from almost nothing.

HENRI FREDERIC AMIEL

Remember that every opportunity has not only a front door, but also a side-door, by which you may enter.

OLIVER WENDALL HOLMES

The greatest secret of success in life is for a person to be ready when their opportunity comes.

BENJAMIN DISRAELI

If I had eight hours to chop down a tree, I'd spend six sharpening my ax.

ABRAHAM LINCOLN

We are all faced
with insurmountable
opportunities.

KOBI YAMADA

I've always believed
that you can funnel good
things toward yourself by
thinking positively.

JIM CARREY

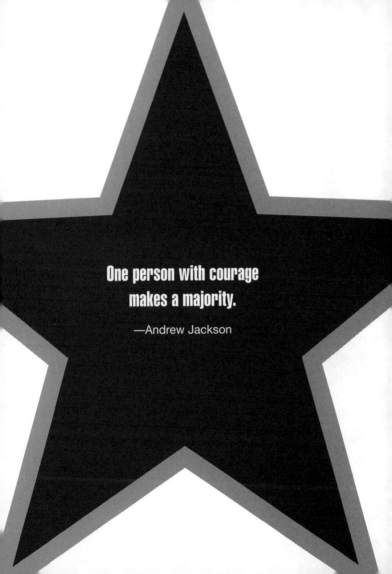

One person with courage
makes a majority.

—Andrew Jackson

Courage is rightly
esteemed the first of
human qualities, because
courage is the quality which
guarantees all others.

WINSTON CHURCHILL

A coward dies a
hundred deaths, a brave
man only once.

HARRY STONE

Abolish fear and
you can accomplish
anything you wish.

DR. C.E. WELCH

Many are called but
few get up.

OLIVER HERFORD

Guts get you there.

B.C. FORBES

★

Do the thing you fear
and the death of fear
is certain.

RALPH WALDO EMERSON

Life shrinks or
expands in proportion
to one's courage.

ANAIS NIN

We are not creatures
of circumstance; we are
creators of circumstance.

BENJAMIN DISRAELI

We have no right
to be cowards.

LEO ROSTEN

★

A great deal of talent is lost
to the world for the want
of a little courage.

SYDNEY SMITH

Strong convictions
precede great actions.

J.F. CLARKE

It takes as much courage
to have tried and failed as
it does to have tried
and succeeded.

ANNE MORROW LINDBERGH

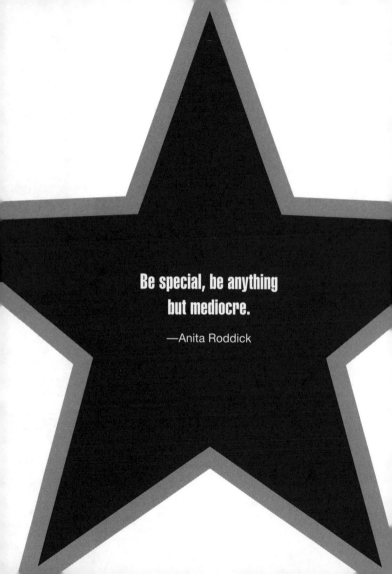

Be special, be anything
but mediocre.

—Anita Roddick

Passion is what
you need to be good,
an unforgiving passion.

DAVID EASTON

This world belongs
to the enthusiastic.

RALPH WALDO EMERSON

In the human heart
new passions are forever
being born; the overthrow
of one almost always means
the rise of another.

LA ROCHEFOUCAULD

I am seeking, I am striving,
I am in it with all my heart.

VINCENT VAN GOGH

Nothing is beneath you
if it's your direction in life.

RALPH WALDO EMERSON

It seems to me we
can never give up longing
and wishing while we are
thoroughly alive. There are
certain things we feel to be
beautiful and good, and we
must hunger after them.

GEORGE ELIOT

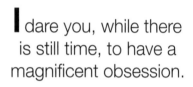

I dare you, while there is still time, to have a magnificent obsession.

WILLIAM DANFORTH

Find the passion. It takes great passion and great energy to do anything creative. I would go so far as to say you can't do it without that passion.

AGNES DEMILLE

Half-heartedness
never won anything.

WILLIAM MCKINLEY

Be fanatics. When it
comes to being, doing
and dreaming the best,
be maniacs.

A. M. ROSENTHAL

I feel sorry for the person who can't get genuinely excited about his work. Not only will he never be satisfied, but he will never achieve anything worthwhile.

WALTER CHRYSLER

Experience teaches us in a millennium what passion teaches us in an hour.

RALPH IRON

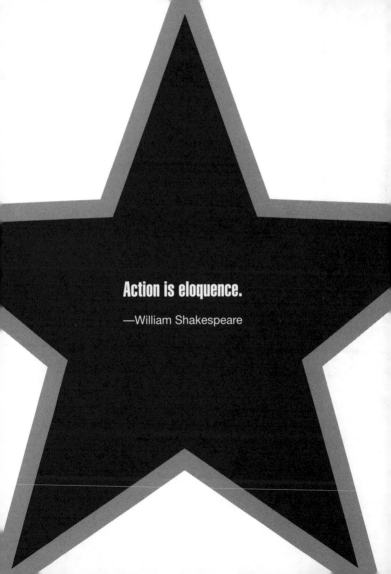

Action is eloquence.

—William Shakespeare

Don't just stand there,
make it happen.

LEE IACOCCA

Decide what you want,
and what you are willing
to exchange for it—
then go to work!

H.L. HUNT

As you grow older, you'll find that the only things you regret are the things you didn't do.

ZACHARY SCOTT

All things come to those who go after them.

ROB ESTES

Humanity falls into
three classes: those who
are immovable, those who
are movable and those
who move!

BENJAMIN FRANKLIN

Nothing risked,
nothing gained.

ALEXANDER WOOLCOTT

Reality always forms
around commitment.

KOBI YAMADA

It is not enough
to stare up the steps,
we must step up
the stairs.

VACLAV HAVEL

There's a big difference between seeing an opportunity and seizing an opportunity.

JIM MOORE

I never worry about action, but only inaction.

F. NIETZSCHE

Success seems to be connected with action. Successful people keep moving. They make mistakes, but they don't quit.

CONRAD HILTON

We believe it is a necessity of our times to translate our beliefs, our hopes and ideals into concrete action.

LENEDRA CAROLL

We never know how
good we are, until we
are called to rise.

EMILY DICKINSON

I am always doing that
which I cannot do, in order
that I may learn how to do it.

PABLO

What isn't tried
won't work.

BERNIE SIEGEL

Success will come to you
in direct proportion to the
number of times you are
willing to risk failure.

EDGE KEYNOTE

Hurdles are in your life for jumping.

—Rev. Sharon Poindexter

Every adversity, every failure, and every heartbreak carries with it the seed of an equivalent or greater benefit.

NAPOLEON HILL

Difficulties exist to be surmounted.

RALPH WALDO EMERSON

When we face the
worst that can happen
in any situation, we grow.
When circumstances are
at their worst, we can
find our best.

ELISABETH KUBLER-ROSS

One who gains strength
by overcoming obstacles
possesses the only strength
which can overcome adversity.

ALBERT SCHWEITZER

There is nothing
we cannot live down,
rise above or overcome.

ELLA WHEELER-WILCOX

When we do face the difficult
times, we need to remember
that circumstances don't make
a person, they reveal a person.

RICHARD CARLSON, PH.D.

Finite to fail,
but infinite to venture.

EMILY DICKINSON

There are really
no bad experiences.
The only bad experiences
are the ones we don't
learn from.

LEO BUSCAGLIA

Trying times
are for trying.

HELEN GAGE DESOTO

I am not concerned
that you have fallen;
I am concerned
that you arise.

ABRAHAM LINCOLN

Failure is only the
opportunity to begin again,
more intelligently.

HENRY FORD

The mere fact that you
have obstacles to overcome
is in your favor.

ROBERT COLLIER

I've failed over and over
and over again in my life.
And that is why I succeed.

MICHAEL JORDAN

You'll never find a
better sparring partner
than adversity.

WALT SCHMIDT

The world is wide, and
I will not waste my life
in friction when it could be
turned into momentum.

FRANCES WILLARD

I have had a lot of success
with failure.

THOMAS EDISON

He who does not tire,
tires adversity.

DIEGO ALVAREZ

We have the ability to
face adversity—to come from
behind and win with grace.

AMBER BROOKMAN

Never give up and never give in.

—Hubert Humphrey

If we're strong enough,
there are no precedents.

F. SCOTT FITZGERALD

When the rock is hard,
we get harder than the rock.
When the job is tough, we get
tougher than the job.

GEORGE CULLUM, SR.

Great works are performed not by strength but by perseverance.

SAMUEL JOHNSON

The difference between the impossible and the possible lies in a person's determination.

TOMMY LASORDA

Things do not happen.
They are made to happen.

JOHN F. KENNEDY

It's the constant and
determined effort that breaks
down all resistance and
sweeps away all obstacles.

CLAUDE M. BRISTOL

Perseverance is not
a long race; it is many short
races one after another.

WALTER ELLIOT

★

It's better to go the extra
foot every time than the
extra mile now and then.

DAN ZADRA

It is by tiny steps
that we ascend to the stars.

JACK LEEDSTROM

Great things are a
series of small things
brought together.

VINCENT VAN GOGH

With ordinary talent and
extraordinary perseverance,
all things are attainable.

THOMAS F. BUXTON

He who has a 'why'
to live for can bear
with any 'how.'

F. NIETZSCHE

Whoever said anybody
has a right to give up?

MARIAN WRIGHT EDELMAN

Instead of 'we almost,'
let the world say about us,
'we did.'

DON WARD

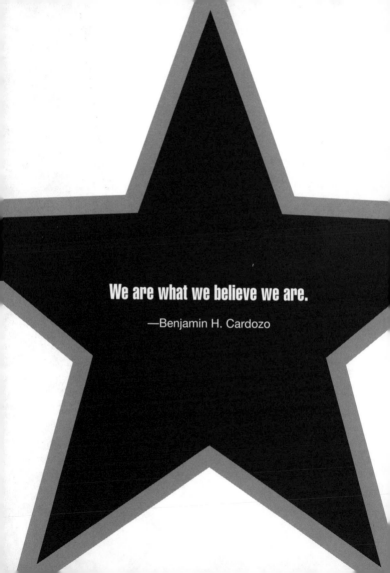

We are what we believe we are.

—Benjamin H. Cardozo

Clear your mind of can't.

SAMUEL JOHNSON

Never let the word
"impossible" stop you from
pursuing what your heart
and spirit urge you to do.
Impossible things come
true every day.

ROBERT K. COOPER

As long as you're worrying about losing what you've got, you'll never be able to see that what's out there waiting for you is a hundred times better!

DON WARD

★

For everything you have missed in life, you have gained something else.

RALPH WALDO EMERSON

Know in your heart that all
things are possible.

LIBBIE FUDIM

Never doubt that a small
group of thoughtful, committed
people can change the world.
Indeed, it is the only thing
that ever has.

MARGARET MEAD

To accomplish
great things, we must
not only plan, but
also believe.

ANATOLE FRANCE

What is now proved
was once only imagined.

WILLIAM BLAKE

What one believes
to be true is either true
or becomes true.

JOHN TILLY

You can do whatever
you have to do, and
sometimes even better
than you think you can.

JIMMY CARTER

To achieve the impossible,
it is precisely the unthinkable
that must be thought.

TOM ROBBINS

The world is divided into
two classes, those who believe
the incredible, and those
who do the improbable.

OSCAR WILDE

It shall be done—
sometime, somewhere.

OPHELIA GUYON BROWNING

After the final no
there comes a yes, and
on that yes the future
world depends.

WALLACE STEVENS

Take charge
of your thoughts.

PLATO

Faith is building on what you
know is here so you can reach
what you know is there.

CULLEN HIGHTOWER

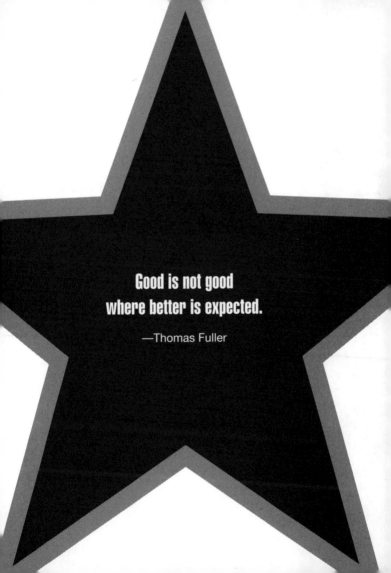

**Good is not good
where better is expected.**

—Thomas Fuller

Amateurs hope.
Professionals make it happen.

GARSON KANIN

If you are prepared, you
have the edge. If you have
the edge, you succeed.

FELICIA MCGRADY

Life is not the way
it's supposed to be.
It's the way it is. The way
you deal with it is what
makes the difference.

VIRGINIA SATIR

Ruthlessly compete
with your own best self.

APOLLO ENGINEERS

It's your life, your one and only life—so take excellence very personally.

SCOTT JOHNSON

The real secret of joy in work is contained in one word—excellence. To know how to do something well is to enjoy it.

PEARL BUCK

By the work
one knows the workman.

JEAN DE LA FONTAINE

The difference between
good and great is just
that little extra effort.

DUFFY DAUGHERTY

Dedication to excellence on any level, in any area, requires an intensity of emotional investment. Unfortunately, there are scores of people who do not make the investment— who do not feel strongly about anything.

THEODORE ISAAC RUBIN

Quality begins with character.

AMOS LAURENCE

Only people
can supply quality.

PHILIP B. CROSBY

Hold yourself to a higher
standard than anybody
else expects of you.

HENRY WARD BEECHER

Failure is impossible.

—Susan B. Anthony

If you are willing,
great things are
possible to you.

GRENVILLE KLEISER

Some succeed because
they are destined to;
most succeed because
they are determined to.

ANATOLE FRANCE

Winners are known
as much by the quality
of their failure as by the
quality of their successes.

MARK MCCORMACK

We are all failures, at least
all the best of us are.

JAMES M. BARRIE

Success is
99 percent failure.

SOICHIRO HONDA

Every day in every way
I'm getting better and better.

EMILE COUE

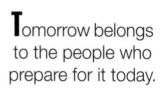

Tomorrow belongs
to the people who
prepare for it today.

MALCOLM X

All things are possible
once you make them so.

JOHANN WOLFGANG VON GOETHE

I don't want to
represent man as he is,
but only as he might be.

ALBERT CAMUS

There's a difference
between what you do
and what you can do.

MARK H. MCCORMACK

There's no grander sight
in the world than that of a
person fired with a great
purpose, dominated by
one unwavering aim.

ORISON SWETT MARDEN

★

There's simply no bona fide,
genuine excuse for not being
super-successful. You control
what you become.

SCOTT ALEXANDER

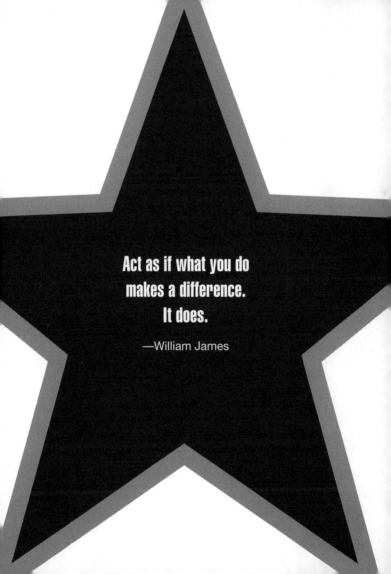

Act as if what you do
makes a difference.
It does.

—William James

It takes courage
for people to listen to
their own goodness
and act on it.

PABLO CASALS

Each time you stand up
for an ideal, you send forth
a tiny ripple of hope.

ROBERT KENNEDY

I am not bound to win,
but I am bound to be true.
I am not bound to succeed,
but I am bound to live up to
what light I might have.

ABRAHAM LINCOLN

The best use of life is
to spend it for something
that will outlast it.

WILLIAM JAMES

Just as there are
no little people or
unimportant lives, there
is no insignificant work.

ELENA BONNER

Destiny is no matter
of chance, it is a matter
of choice.

WILLIAM JENNINGS BRYAN

Whatever you are meant
to do, move toward it and
it will come to you.

GLORIA DUNN

We write our own destiny.
We become what we do.

MADAME CHIANG KAI-SHEK

Through reverence
for life I raise my existence
to its highest value and
offer it to the world.

ALBERT SCHWEITZER

Our deeds follow us,
and what we have been
makes us what we are.

JOHN DYKES

One by one,
we can be the
better world we wish for.

KOBI YAMADA

The influence of each
human on others in this life
is a kind of immortality.

JOHN QUINCY ADAMS

At the end of life, our
questions are very simple.
Did I live fully?
Did I love well?

JACK KORNFIELD

Think beyond your lifetime
if you want to accomplish
something truly worthwhile.

WALT DISNEY

When we strive
to become better than we are,
everything around us becomes
better, too.

HEIDI WILLS

We find what we search for—
or, if we don't find it,
we become it.

JESSAMYN WEST

STAR ★ SERIES

Also available from
Compendium Publishing
are these spirited companion
books in the Star Series
of great quotations:

GOALS

LEADERSHIP

TEAMWORK

These books may be ordered directly
from the publisher (800) 914-3327.
But please try your local bookstore first!

www.compendiuminc.com